Highlights

Highlights of GAO-10-972, a report to congressional requesters

September 2010

INFORMATION SHARING

Federal Agencies Are Helping Fusion Centers Build and Sustain Capabilities and Protect Privacy, but Could Better Measure Results

I0409697

Why GAO Did This Study

Recent terrorist activity, such as the attempted Times Square bombing, underscores the need for terrorism-related information sharing. Since 2001, all 50 states and some local governments have established fusion centers, where homeland security, terrorism, and other intelligence information is shared. The federal government recognizes the importance of fusion centers; however, as GAO reported in October 2007, centers face challenges in sustaining their operations. GAO was asked to assess the extent to which (1) the Department of Homeland Security (DHS) has taken action to support fusion centers' efforts to maintain and grow their operations, and (2) DHS and the Department of Justice (DOJ) have supported fusion centers in establishing privacy and civil liberties protections. GAO reviewed relevant legislation and federal guidance; conducted interviews with 14 of 72 fusion centers, selected on the basis of location and time in operation, among other factors; and interviewed DHS and DOJ officials. The views of fusion center officials are not generalizable but provided insights.

What GAO Recommends

GAO recommends that DHS define steps to develop and implement standard performance measures for centers and commit to a timeframe for completing them. DHS concurred and described steps it is taking to address the recommendation.

View GAO-10-972 or key components.
For more information, contact Eileen Larence at (202) 512-8777 or larencee@gao.gov.

What GAO Found

Fusion centers have cited DHS grant funding as critical to achieving the baseline capabilities—the standards the government and fusion centers have defined as necessary for centers to be considered capable of performing basic functions in the national information sharing network, such as standards related to information gathering and intelligence analysis. However, DHS has not set standard performance measures for the centers. Fusion centers nationwide reported that federal funding accounted for about 61 percent of their total fiscal year 2010 budgets, but DHS's Homeland Security Grant Program (HSGP), the primary grant program through which fusion centers receive funding, is not specifically focused on, or limited to, fusion centers. Rather, states and local governments determine the amount of HSGP funding they allocate to fusion centers each year from among a number of competing homeland security needs. As a result, fusion centers continue to raise concerns about the lack of a longer-term, predictable federal funding source. DHS, in coordination with the Program Manager for the Information Sharing Environment and DOJ, has a nationwide assessment of centers' baseline capabilities under way. To be completed in October 2010, the goal of the assessment is to provide federal agencies and fusion centers with more accurate information on the status of centers' abilities, help identify gaps between centers' current operations and the baseline capabilities, and use this information to develop strategies and realign resources to close those gaps going forward. Recent federal guidance also requires that, by October 29, 2010, DHS should develop an annual reporting process that will document the total operational and sustainment costs of each of the 72 fusion centers in the national network so as to assess the adequacy of current funding mechanisms. If centers are to receive continued federal financial support, it is important that they are also able to demonstrate their impact and value added to the nation's information sharing goals. However, there are no standard performance measures across all fusion centers to do this. DHS has not started developing such measures because the agency is currently focusing on completing the nationwide assessment and compiling its results and, as such, has not defined next steps or target timeframes for designing and implementing these measures. Defining the steps it will take to design and implement a set of measures and committing to a target timeframe for their completion could better position DHS to demonstrate the value and impact of the national network of fusion centers.

To help fusion centers develop privacy and civil liberties policies and protections, DHS and DOJ have provided technical assistance and training, including a template on which to base a privacy and civil liberties policy, and a joint process for reviewing fusion centers' policies to ensure they are consistent with federal requirements. The 14 centers GAO interviewed were at different stages of the policy review process, with 7 completed as of June 2010. Officials from all 14 of the fusion centers GAO interviewed stated that the guidance DHS and DOJ provided was helpful and integral in assisting them to draft their policies.

_____ United States Government Accountability Office

Contents

Abbreviations

ACLU	American Civil Liberties Union
CLIA	Civil Liberties Impact Assessment
CRS	Congressional Research Service
CRCL	Office for Civil Rights and Civil Liberties
DHS	Department of Homeland Security
DOJ	Department of Justice
FBI	Federal Bureau of Investigation
FEMA	Federal Emergency Management Agency
HSGP	Homeland Security Grant Program
I&A	Office of Intelligence and Analysis
ISE	Information Sharing Environment
NFCA	National Fusion Center Association
PIA	Privacy Impact Assessment
PM-ISE	Program Manager for the ISE
SAA	State Administrative Agency
SLPO	State and Local Program Office

United States Government Accountability Office
Washington, DC 20548

September 29, 2010

The Honorable Mark Pryor
Chairman
The Honorable John Ensign
Ranking Member
Subcommittee on State, Local, and Private
    Sector Preparedness and Integration
Committee on Homeland Security and Governmental Affairs
United States Senate

The Honorable Tom Coburn
United States Senate

Recent terrorist activity, such as the attempted Times Square bombing and the attempted bombing of Northwest Airlines Flight 253, emphasizes the importance of developing a national information sharing capability to efficiently and expeditiously gather, analyze, and disseminate law enforcement, homeland security, public safety, and terrorism information. Since 2001, all 50 states and some local governments have established fusion centers to address gaps in terrorism-related information sharing that the federal government cannot address alone and provide a mechanism for information sharing within the state. Although fusion centers vary because they were primarily established to meet state and local needs, under federal law, a fusion center is defined as a collaborative effort of two or more federal, state, local, or tribal government agencies that combines resources, expertise, or information with the goal of maximizing the ability of such agencies to detect, prevent, investigate, apprehend, and respond to criminal or terrorist activity. As of August 2010, there were 72 fusion centers nationwide.[1] Fusion centers are a component of the nation's Information Sharing Environment (ISE), which was established by the Intelligence Reform and Terrorism Prevention Act of

---

[1] All 50 states have designated a primary fusion center to serve as the focal point for information sharing. In general, these fusion centers are statewide in jurisdiction and are operated by state entities, such as the state police or bureau of investigation. In addition, 22 major urban areas have established their own fusion centers, which are regional centers that usually cover large cities with substantial populations and numerous critical infrastructure sites and may be operated by city or county law enforcement or emergency management agencies. For purposes of this report, "fusion centers" is used to refer to both state and major urban area fusion centers.

2004 (Intelligence Reform Act) to facilitate information sharing, access, and collaboration in order to combat terrorism more effectively.[2]

The Implementing Recommendations of the 9/11 Commission Act of 2007 (9/11 Commission Act) requires the Secretary of Homeland Security, in consultation with others, to establish a state, local, and regional fusion center initiative within the Department of Homeland Security (DHS) to establish partnerships with fusion centers.[3] Through the initiative, DHS is required to provide to fusion centers operational and intelligence advice and assistance, as well as management assistance, and facilitate close communication and coordination between fusion centers and DHS. In addition, the initiative is to provide training to fusion centers and encourage the centers to participate in terrorism-threat-related exercises conducted by DHS. Accordingly, the federal government has recognized that fusion centers represent a critical source of local information about potential threats for federal agencies and a mechanism for these agencies to disseminate terrorism-related information and intelligence. DHS, the Department of Justice (DOJ), and the Program Manager for the ISE (PM-ISE) have taken steps to partner with and leverage fusion centers as part of the overall ISE. Further, the National Strategy for Information Sharing (National Strategy) states that fusion centers will serve as the primary focal points within states and localities for the receipt and sharing of terrorism-related information. Through the National Strategy, the federal government is promoting fusion centers to achieve a baseline level of capability and to ensure compliance with all applicable privacy laws and standards to become interconnected with the federal government and each other in a national network capable of sharing terrorism-related information.

In January 2005, we designated information sharing for homeland security a high-risk area because the government had continued to face formidable

---

[2]Pub. L. No. 108-458, 118 Stat. 3664, as amended. This act also required, among other things, that the President designate a Program Manager with governmentwide authority to manage the ISE, oversee its implementation, assist in the development of ISE standards and practices, and monitor and assess its implementation by federal agencies. § 1016(f), 118 Stat. at 3667-68. The President was also required to issue guidelines, in consultation with the Privacy and Civil Liberties Oversight Board, which protect privacy and civil liberties in the development of the ISE, and submit a report to Congress describing the means that privacy and civil liberties will be protected in the ISE. § 1016(d)(2)(A), (e)(8), 118 Stat. at 3665-67.

[3]Pub. L. No. 110-53, § 511, 121 Stat. 266, 317-324.

challenges in analyzing and disseminating this information in a timely, accurate, and useful manner. We reported that information is a crucial tool in fighting terrorism and that its timely dissemination is critical to maintaining the security of our nation. This area remained on the high-risk list for our January 2009 update.[4] In 2007, we reviewed the status of fusion centers nationwide and reported that fusion center officials faced challenges in obtaining and maintaining the funding and personnel necessary to conduct their operations.[5] According to the officials, uncertainties in the amount of federal grant funding to be allocated from year to year made it difficult to plan for the future and created concerns about the centers' ability to sustain their capability for the long-term. To improve efforts to create a national network of fusion centers, we recommended that the federal government should articulate its role in supporting fusion centers and determine whether it expects to provide resources to centers over the long-term to help ensure their sustainability. DHS and the PM-ISE concurred with our recommendation, stating that recent efforts to define DHS's, and the federal government's, roles and responsibilities in supporting the development of the nationwide network of fusion centers demonstrates a long-term commitment to helping to ensure their sustainability.[6] However, federal, state, and local entities continue to raise concerns about fusion centers' ability to maintain their operations with limited or uncertain federal grant funding, especially as many state and local governments face near-term and long-term fiscal challenges.

In addition, the 9/11 Commission Act requires the Secretary of Homeland Security, in consultation with the Attorney General, to establish guidelines that include standards for fusion centers related to the privacy of information. For example, these standards are to include that any fusion center shall develop, publish, and adhere to a privacy and civil liberties policy consistent with federal, state, and local law. Because fusion centers collect, analyze, and disseminate information on potential criminal and terrorist threats, some entities have raised concerns that centers are susceptible to privacy and civil liberties violations. For example, according to the American Civil Liberties Union (ACLU), the fusion center concept

---

[4]GAO, *High-Risk Series: An Update*, GAO-09-271 (Washington, D.C.: January 2009).

[5]GAO, *Homeland Security: Federal Efforts Are Helping to Alleviate Some Challenges Encountered by State and Local Information Fusion Centers*, GAO-08-35 (Washington, D.C.: Oct. 30, 2007).

[6]DOJ did not provide comments on our recommendation.

encourages state and local law enforcement personnel to gather intelligence that could potentially lead to violations of citizens' rights to privacy and civil liberties. According to a senior DOJ official, such violations by fusion centers could lead to a loss of public support or confidence in fusion centers, harm to individuals, proliferation of inaccurate data, or liability. In light of these risks, questions remain about how centers are implementing privacy and civil liberties policies to ensure that centers handle information in a manner that protects citizens' constitutional rights.

Considering these issues and the fusion centers' role in the ISE, you asked us to provide Congress with an assessment of the current status of fusion centers' efforts to maintain and grow their operations and establish privacy and civil liberties protections with support from the federal government. Specifically, this report addresses the following questions:

- To what extent has DHS taken action to support fusion centers' efforts to maintain and grow their operations?
- To what extent are DHS and DOJ supporting fusion centers in establishing privacy and civil liberties protections?

To assess the extent to which DHS has supported centers in their efforts, we analyzed relevant laws and strategies, such as the 9/11 Commission Act and the National Strategy, related to fusion centers' role in the ISE and federal efforts to support centers. We also examined guidance, such as the Baseline Capabilities for State and Major Urban Area Fusion Centers (Baseline Capabilities), which describes the minimum capabilities and operational standards necessary for fusion centers.[7] We focused our review on DHS's efforts because DHS is the Executive Agent in managing federal interaction with fusion centers and is to coordinate its efforts with DOJ and the PM-ISE. To obtain fusion center views, we conducted interviews with officials from a non-probability sample of 14 of 72 fusion

---

[7]Global Justice Information Sharing Initiative, *Baseline Capabilities for State and Major Urban Area Fusion Centers, A Supplement to the Fusion Center Guidelines* (September 2008).

centers.[8] We selected these centers to reflect a range of characteristics, including whether the center is a state or major urban area fusion center; length of time in operation; geographic region;[9] and fiscal year 2010 funding allocations for the centers' states or urban areas from the DHS Homeland Security Grant Program (HSGP), which is the primary federal grant program through which fusion centers may receive funding. Specifically, we interviewed fusion center directors, or their designees, to obtain information on their centers' approaches and plans to sustain operations, and their perspectives on federal efforts to support these approaches as well as any challenges or issues encountered in sustaining operations. While their comments cannot be generalized to all fusion centers nationwide, the interviews provided a range of perspectives and useful insights on the issue of sustainability.

To assess DHS support provided to fusion centers, we examined guidance, such as for the DHS Fiscal Year 2010 HSGP. We also analyzed documents, such as program descriptions, related to federal efforts to assess fusion centers' baseline capabilities and provide training, technical assistance, and grant funding. We interviewed officials from DHS's Office of Intelligence and Analysis (I&A), which oversees the fusion center program; DHS's Federal Emergency Management Agency's (FEMA) Grant Programs Directorate and Office of Counterterrorism and Security Preparedness within Protection and National Preparedness, which administer the HSGP and provide support to fusion centers; DOJ's Office of Justice Programs, which provides training and technical assistance to centers; the Federal Bureau of Investigation (FBI), which provides personnel and support to centers; and the Office of the PM-ISE, which oversees management of the ISE. We discussed plans and efforts related to establishing performance measures for fusion centers and compared these

---

[8]We interviewed officials from the following 14 centers: Arkansas State Fusion Center; Boston Regional Intelligence Center; Delaware Information and Analysis Center; Georgia Information Sharing and Analysis Center; Kansas City Regional Terrorism Early Warning Group, Inter-Agency Analysis Center; Los Angeles Joint Regional Intelligence Center/Los Angeles Regional Terrorism Threat Assessment Center; New York State Intelligence Center; Northern California Regional Intelligence Center; Oklahoma Information Fusion Center; Southern Nevada Counterterrorism Center; Southeastern Wisconsin Threat Analysis Center; Tennessee Fusion Center; Virginia Fusion Center; and the Wisconsin Statewide Information Center.

[9]Specifically, we selected fusion centers whose directors were identified as the chair or co-chair of a regional fusion center group. DHS and DOJ established regional groups (i.e., western, central, southeast, and northeast) in order to facilitate interaction among fusion centers in the same area and communication with federal partners.

plans with criteria in standard practices for program management.[10] In addition, we conducted interviews with the National Fusion Center Association (NFCA), a nonprofit association that represents the interests of fusion centers, to obtain a broad perspective on fusion center sustainability and the role of DHS, DOJ, and the PM-ISE in supporting centers' efforts. Lastly, we attended the 2010 National Fusion Center Conference to obtain information about federal plans and efforts to support centers and issues and concerns of centers nationwide.[11]

To assess the extent to which DHS and DOJ are supporting fusion centers in establishing privacy and civil liberties protections, we analyzed relevant statutes, including the 9/11 Commission Act and the Intelligence Reform Act, and guidance, such as the ISE Privacy Guidelines, Baseline Capabilities, and DHS HSGP guidance to identify required and recommended actions for fusion centers to take to establish these protections.[12] We analyzed plans and documentation, such as the DHS Privacy Office's 2008 Privacy Impact Assessment of fusion centers and privacy-related training and technical assistance materials. We also assessed the DHS and DOJ Fusion Center Privacy, Civil Rights, and Civil Liberties Policy Template, which is intended to assist fusion center personnel in developing their privacy and civil liberties policies. We compared this template against the ISE Privacy Guidelines to determine the extent to which the template included components of that guidance. In addition, we interviewed officials from DHS's Privacy Office, DHS's Office for Civil Rights and Civil Liberties (CRCL), DOJ's Office of Privacy and Civil Liberties, and the PM-ISE about efforts to review centers' policies, the status of centers' policy development, privacy-related training and technical assistance, and plans for supporting fusion centers' implementation of privacy and civil liberties protections. We also interviewed representatives from the Institute for Intergovernmental Research, the DOJ contractor that reviews fusion centers' privacy and civil liberties policies, to obtain additional information about the review

---

[10]Program management standards we reviewed are reflected in the Project Management Institute's *The Standard for Program Management* © (2006).

[11]The 2010 National Fusion Center Conference was sponsored by the PM-ISE, DHS, and DOJ, among others. The conference brought together close to 1,000 state, local, tribal, territorial, and federal partners involved in state and major urban area fusion centers across the country, including fusion center directors and senior leadership.

[12]In 2006, the PM-ISE issued the ISE Privacy Guidelines, which outline guidelines and steps for ISE members to implement to protect the information privacy rights and civil liberties of Americans.

process and any challenges encountered related to the development of these policies.[13] To describe steps fusion centers are taking to establish privacy and civil liberties protections, we included questions in our interviews with officials from 14 fusion centers about the development of privacy and civil liberties policies and procedures; support provided by DHS, DOJ, and the PM-ISE; and any challenges or issues encountered in establishing the protections. Lastly, we included questions in our interviews with NFCA and ACLU officials to obtain a broad perspective on privacy issues in fusion centers.

We conducted this performance audit from March 2010 through September 2010 in accordance with generally accepted government auditing standards. Those standards require that we plan and perform the audit to obtain sufficient, appropriate evidence to provide a reasonable basis for our findings and conclusions based on our audit objectives. We believe that the evidence obtained provides a reasonable basis for our findings and conclusions based on our audit objectives.

Background

Fusion Centers

Nationwide, states and major urban areas have established fusion centers to coordinate the gathering, analysis, and dissemination of law enforcement, homeland security, public safety, and terrorism information. After centers had begun to be established around the country, Congress passed the 9/11 Commission Act to require the Secretary of Homeland Security to share information with and support fusion centers. The National Strategy identifies fusion centers as vital assets critical to sharing information related to terrorism because they serve as focal points for the two-way exchange of information between federal agencies and state and local governments. According to DHS, fusion centers are the primary way that DHS shares intelligence and analysis with state and local homeland security agencies. For example, fusion centers typically issue analytical products, such as daily or weekly bulletins on general criminal or intelligence information and intelligence assessments which, in general, provide in-depth reporting on an emerging threat, group, or crime. These

---

[13]The Institute for Intergovernmental Research is a nonprofit research and training organization that specializes in law enforcement, juvenile justice, criminal justice, and homeland security issues.

products are primarily created for law enforcement entities and other community partners, such as members of the critical infrastructure sectors. In recent years, fusion centers have been credited with being influential in disrupting a planned terrorist attack on the New York City subway system, investigating bomb threats against U.S. airlines, and providing intelligence support to several political conventions and summits. Other fusion centers have been instrumental in providing intelligence and analytical support to assist with securing our nation's borders. For example, the Arizona Counterterrorism Information Center and the New York State Intelligence Center routinely (i.e., either twice a week or quarterly, respectively) issue border-specific intelligence products to enhance the situational awareness of law enforcement agencies in border communities.

While all fusion centers were generally created by state and local governments to improve information sharing across levels of government and to prevent terrorism or other threats, the missions of fusion centers vary based on the environment in which the center operates. Some fusion centers have adopted an "all-crimes" approach, incorporating information on terrorism and other high-risk threats into their jurisdiction's existing law enforcement framework to ensure that possible precursor crimes, such as counterfeiting or narcotics smuggling, are screened and analyzed for linkages to terrorist planning or other criminal activity. Other fusion centers have adopted an "all-hazards" approach. In addition to collecting, analyzing, and disseminating information on potential terrorist planning and other crimes, these fusion centers identify and prioritize types of major disasters and emergencies, such as hurricanes or earthquakes, which could occur within their jurisdiction. In doing so, they gather, analyze, and disseminate information to assist relevant responsible agencies—law enforcement, fire, public health, emergency management, critical infrastructure—with the prevention, protection, response, or recovery efforts of those incidents.

Fusion centers also vary in their personnel composition and staffing levels. Consistent with the statutory definition of a fusion center, these centers typically bring together in one location representatives from several different state or local agencies, such as state and local law enforcement agencies—state police, county sheriffs, and city police departments—homeland security agencies, emergency management agencies, and the National Guard. In addition, as DHS is required to the maximum extent possible to assign officers and intelligence analysts to fusion centers, many centers have federal personnel working on-site, such as DHS intelligence operations specialists and Customs and Border Protection agents, along with others such as FBI intelligence analysts and Drug Enforcement Administration agents. In terms of staffing levels, a 2009 joint DHS and PM-ISE survey of fusion centers reported that the number of personnel working at these centers ranged from under 10 employees to over 75 per center, as shown in figure 1.

Figure 1: Staffing Levels Reported by 62 of 72 Fusion Centers, as of March 2009

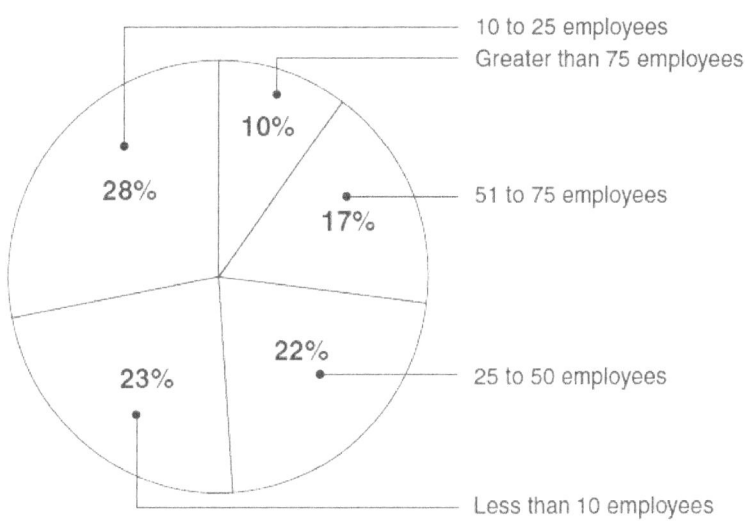

Source: GAO (presentation), PM-ISE (data).

Note: Information was aggregated, but not verified by the PM-ISE or GAO.

Federal Role in Relation to Fusion Centers

Recognizing that DHS had already begun to provide support to fusion centers but needed to play a stronger, more constructive role in assisting these centers, Congress passed the 9/11 Commission Act, which required the Secretary of Homeland Security to create the State, Local, and Regional Fusion Center Initiative. [14] The Act also required the Secretary, in coordination with representatives from fusion centers and the states, to take certain actions in support of the initiative. Specifically, the Act requires that the Secretary take a number of steps to support the centers, including supporting efforts to integrate fusion centers into the ISE, assigning personnel to centers, incorporating fusion center intelligence information into DHS information, providing training, and facilitating close

[14] In consultation with the PM-ISE and the Attorney General, as well as the department's Privacy Officer, Officer for Civil Rights and Civil Liberties, and Privacy and Civil Liberties Oversight Board.

GAO-10-972 Fusion Centers

communication and coordination between the centers and DHS, among others. The law also required the Secretary to issue guidance that includes standards that fusion centers shall undertake certain activities. These include, for example, that centers collaboratively develop a mission statement, identify expectations and goals, measure performance, and determine center effectiveness; create a collaborative environment for the sharing of intelligence and information among federal, state, local, and tribal government agencies, the private sector, and the public, consistent with guidance from the President and the PM-ISE; and offer a variety of intelligence and information services and products.

DHS has taken steps to organize and establish a management structure to coordinate its support of fusion centers. In June 2006, DHS tasked I&A with the responsibility for managing DHS's support to fusion centers. I&A established a State and Local Program Office (SLPO) as the focal point for supporting fusion center operations and to maximize state and local capabilities to detect, prevent, and respond to terrorist and homeland security threats.

Consistent with the 9/11 Commission Act and Intelligence Reform Act, DHS, in conjunction with DOJ and the PM-ISE, has issued a series of guidance documents to support fusion centers in establishing their operations. In 2006, through the Global Justice Information Sharing Initiative (Global), DHS and DOJ jointly issued the Fusion Center Guidelines, a document that outlines 18 recommended elements for establishing and operating fusion centers consistently across the country, such as establishing and maintaining a center based on funding availability and sustainability; ensuring personnel are properly trained; and developing, publishing, and adhering to a privacy and civil liberties policy.[15]

To supplement the Fusion Center Guidelines, in September 2008, DHS, DOJ, and Global jointly published the Baseline Capabilities, which were developed in collaboration with the PM-ISE and other federal, state, and local officials. The Baseline Capabilities define the capabilities needed to achieve a national, integrated network of fusion centers and detail the

---

[15]Global serves as a Federal Advisory Committee and advises the U.S. Attorney General on justice information sharing and integration initiatives. Global was created to support the broad exchange of justice and public safety information and consists of organizations and federal, state, and local agencies from a range of law enforcement, judicial, and correctional disciplines.

GAO-10-972 Fusion Centers

standards necessary for a fusion center to be considered capable of performing basic functions by the fusion center community. For example, the Baseline Capabilities include standards for fusion centers related to information gathering, recognition of indicators and warnings, processing information, intelligence analysis and production, and intelligence and information dissemination. In addition, the Baseline Capabilities include standards for the management and administrative functioning of a fusion center. Among these are standards for ensuring information privacy and civil liberties protections, developing a training plan for personnel, and establishing information technology and communications infrastructure to ensure seamless communication between center personnel and partners. The development of these baseline standards is called for in the National Strategy, which identifies their development as a key step to reaching a national integrated network of fusion centers. By achieving this baseline level of capability, it is intended that a fusion center will have the necessary structures, processes, and tools in place to support the gathering, processing, analysis, and dissemination of terrorism, homeland security, and law enforcement information.

In accordance with the 9/11 Commission Act, DHS, DOJ, and the PM-ISE rely on fusion centers as critical nodes in the nation's homeland security strategy and provide them with a variety of other support.

- Federal Grant Funding: DHS's HSGP awards funds to states, territories, and urban areas to enhance their ability to prepare for, prevent, protect against, respond to, and recover from terrorist attacks and other major disasters.[16] The fiscal year 2010 HSGP consists of five separate programs, two of which are primarily used by states and local jurisdictions, at their discretion, for fusion-center-related funding.[17] These grant programs are

---

[16]DHS's FEMA, specifically the Grant Programs Directorate within Protection and National Preparedness, manages the grant process and allocates these funds to state and local entities.

[17]The State Homeland Security Program supports the implementation of State Homeland Security Strategies to address planning, organization, equipment, training, and exercise needs to prevent, protect against, respond to, and recover from acts of terrorism and other catastrophic events. Each state receives a minimum allocation under this program and additional funds are allocated based on the analysis of risk and anticipated effectiveness. The Urban Area Security Initiative program addresses the planning, organization, equipment, training, and exercise needs of high-threat, high-density urban areas, and assists them in building an enhanced and sustainable capacity to prevent, protect against, respond to, and recover from acts of terrorism. These funds are allocated on the basis of risk and anticipated effectiveness to about 64 candidate areas.

not specifically focused on, or limited to, fusion centers. Thus, fusion centers do not receive direct, dedicated funding from DHS; rather, the amount of grant funding a fusion center receives is determined by a state's State Administrative Agency (SAA)—the state-level agency responsible for managing all homeland security grants and associated program requirements—or an urban area's working group, which has similar responsibilities. A fusion center typically contributes to the development of a state's federal grant application by providing information on how it will use the proposed funding needed, called an investment justification.

- Personnel: DHS and DOJ have deployed, or assigned, either part-time or full-time personnel to fusion centers to support their operations and serve as liaisons between the fusion center and federal components. For example, DHS personnel are to assist the center in using ISE information; review information provided by state, local, and tribal personnel; create products derived from this information and other DHS homeland security information; and assist in disseminating these products. As of July 2010, DHS's I&A had deployed 58 intelligence officers and the FBI had deployed 74 special agents and analysts full time to 38 of the 72 fusion centers.

- Access to Information and Systems: DHS and DOJ also share classified and unclassified homeland security and terrorism information with fusion centers through several information technology networks and systems. For example, in February 2010, DHS's I&A reported that it had installed the Homeland Secure Data Network, which supports the sharing of federal secret-level intelligence and information with state, local, and tribal partners, at 33 of 72 fusion centers. DHS also provides an unclassified network, the Homeland Security Information Network, which allows federal, state, and local homeland security and terrorism-related information sharing.

- Training and Technical Assistance: DHS has partnered with DOJ, through Global, to offer fusion centers a variety of training and technical assistance programs. These include training on intelligence analysis and privacy and civil liberties protections, as well as technical assistance with technology implementation, security, and the development of liaison programs to coordinate with other state and local agencies.

Privacy Requirements for Fusion Centers

Fusion centers have a number of privacy related requirements. As provided under the 9/11 Commission Act, DHS is required to issue standards that fusion centers are to develop, publish, and adhere to a privacy and civil liberties policy consistent with federal, state, and local law. In addition, the standards must provide that a fusion center give appropriate privacy and civil liberties training to all state, local, tribal, and private sector representatives at the center and have appropriate security measures in place for the facility, data, and personnel. Because fusion centers are within the ISE when they access certain kinds of information, federal law requires they adhere to ISE privacy standards issued by the President or the PM-ISE under the authority of the Intelligence Reform Act, as amended. Other federal requirements found in 28 C.F.R. part 23, Criminal Intelligence Systems Operating Policies, apply to federally funded criminal intelligence systems, and fusion centers receiving criminal intelligence information must follow these procedures, which also include privacy requirements.

In 2006, the PM-ISE issued the ISE Privacy Guidelines, which establish a framework for sharing information in the ISE in a manner that protects privacy and other legal rights. The ISE Privacy Guidelines apply to federal departments and agencies and, therefore, do not directly impose obligations on state and local government entities. However, the ISE Privacy Guidelines do require federal agencies and the PM-ISE to work with nonfederal entities, such as fusion centers, seeking to access protected information to ensure that the entities develop and implement appropriate policies and procedures that are at least as comprehensive as those contained in the ISE Privacy Guidelines.[18] Among the primary components of these guidelines, agencies are required to, for example, ensure that protected information is used only for authorized, specific purposes; properly identify any privacy-protected information to be shared; put in place security, accountability, and audit mechanisms; facilitate the prevention and correction of any errors in protected information; and document privacy and civil liberties protections in a privacy and civil liberties policy.

---

[18]Protected information is information about U.S. citizens and lawful permanent residents that is subject to information privacy or other legal protections under the U.S. Constitution and federal laws.

Federal Efforts Are Under Way to Assess Centers' Capabilities, Target Funding to Capability Gaps, and Assess Costs, but Measuring Results Achieved Could Help Show Centers' Value to the ISE

Officials in all 14 fusion centers we contacted cited federal funding as critical to expanding their operations and achieving and maintaining the baseline capabilities needed to sustain the national network of fusion centers. An assessment of fusion centers, led by the PM-ISE, DHS, and DOJ, is under way to obtain data about the current capabilities of centers nationwide, identify the operational gaps that remain, and determine what resources centers may need to close the gaps. DHS is evaluating whether to amend its grant guidance to require fusion centers to use future funding to support efforts to meet and maintain the baseline capabilities. DHS also has plans to assess the costs of the fusion center network to help inform decisions about the extent to which the funding mechanisms in place in support of fusion centers are adequate, or if other funding avenues need to be explored. However, taking steps to implement standard performance measures to track the results of fusion centers' efforts to support information sharing and assess the impact of their operations could help demonstrate center value to the ISE and enable the federal government to justify and prioritize future resources in support of the national network.

Fusion Center Officials We Interviewed Cited Federal Funding as Critical to Sustaining Operations

Officials in all 14 fusion centers we contacted stated that without continued federal grant funding, in particular DHS grant funding, their centers would not be able to expand, or in some instances even maintain, operations. States have reported to DHS that they have used about $426 million in grant funding from fiscal year 2004 through 2009 to support fusion-related activities nationwide, as shown in table 1.

Table 1: DHS Funding Reported by Grantees to Support Fusion Center Activities, Fiscal Years 2004 through 2009

Fiscal year	Funding reported by grantees to support fusion center activities
2004	$100,320,799
2005	57,246,542
2006	62,664,343
2007	78,723,783
2008	61,864,080
2009	65,402,360
Total	$426,221,907

Source: DHS.

Note: Data are as of June 16, 2010, and include all FEMA preparedness grant programs. Figures represent activities aligned to project types that support fusion center activities, such as the following: establish/enhance a terrorism intelligence/early warning system, center, or task force; establish/enhance public-private emergency preparedness program; and develop/enhance homeland security/emergency management organization and structure. Data are self-reported by grantees every 6 months, and according to FEMA officials, are not validated to ensure that funds were exclusively used to support fusion center activities.

According to a nationwide survey conducted by DHS and the PM-ISE, of the 52 of 72 fusion centers that responded, on average, over half of their 2010 budgets were supported by federal funding.[19] Specifically, as shown in figure 2, these centers reported that federal grant funding accounted for 61 percent of their total current budgets of about $102 million and state or local funds accounted for 39 percent ($40 million), according to information reported to DHS and the PM-ISE.[20] For the 14 centers we contacted, officials in 6 of the centers reported relying on federal grant funding for more than 50 percent of their annual budgets, which ranged from $600,000 to about $16 million.[21]

[19]This figure is based on information reported to the PM-ISE by 52 of 72 fusion centers. Information was aggregated, but not verified, by PM-ISE or GAO.

[20]While the average overall current fiscal year fusion center budget was just under $2.1 million, the centers' budgets varied in size. For example, 52 percent of the centers reported current fiscal year budgets of $1 million or more, while 48 percent reported current fiscal year budgets of less than $1 million.

[21]These figures are based on estimated annual operating budgets as reported to us by officials from the 14 fusion centers we interviewed. We did not independently verify the accuracy of these estimates.

Figure 2: Average Funding Breakdown for Fiscal Year 2010 Budgets Reported by 52 of 72 Fusion Centers

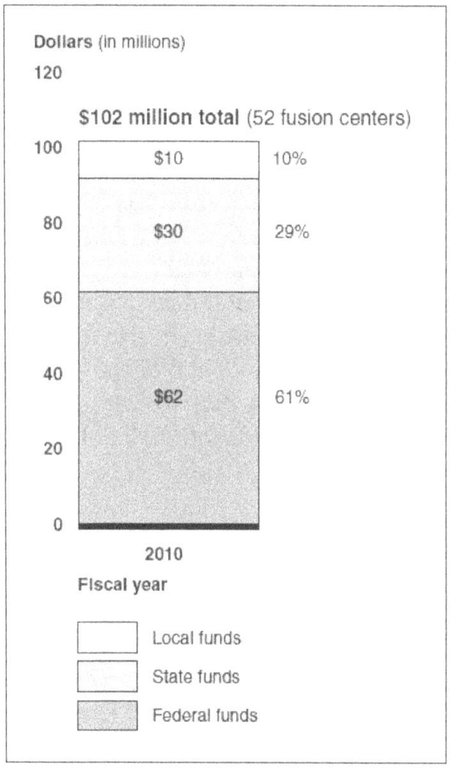

Dollars (in millions)

120

$102 million total (52 fusion centers)

100 | $10 | 10%

80 | $30 | 29%

60

40 | $62 | 61%

20

0

2010
Fiscal year

☐ Local funds
☐ State funds
▨ Federal funds

Source: GAO (presentation), PM-ISE (data).

Note: Above amounts rounded to the nearest whole number. Information was aggregated, but not verified by the PM-ISE or GAO.

Officials in all 14 of the centers we contacted stated that federal funding was critical to long-term sustainability and provided varying examples of the impact that not having federal grant funding would have on their fusion centers. Officials in four fusion centers stated that without federal funding, their centers would not be able to continue operations. For example, an official in one of these centers stated that with the state's economic recession, the fusion center does not expect to grow operations over the next 5 years and is struggling to maintain the personnel and funding needed to maintain their current operations, which includes fewer than 10 full-time personnel with an estimated budget of a little over $500,000. Officials in another fusion center stated that while they have a comparatively large budget of about $10 million, they could not maintain their level of operations without the federal grant funding, about $5 million per year, they receive.

Fusion Centers See Federal Funding as Necessary to Achieve and Maintain the Baseline Capabilities; a Nationwide Assessment to Gauge Gaps in Centers' Capabilities Is Under Way

Officials in all 14 fusion centers we contacted stated that without sustained federal funding, centers could not expand operations to close the gaps between their current operations and the baseline capabilities, negatively affecting their ability to function as part of the national network. For example, officials from one fusion center stated that they currently do not have the resources to hire a security officer, which affects the center's development, implementation, maintenance, and oversight of security measures, including ensuring that security measures are in place to provide the proper information protection in compliance with all applicable laws and the center's privacy and civil liberties policy. Officials in another fusion center stated that federal grant funding is essential to expanding their outreach and coordination with other state and local entities—a recommended baseline capability and one of the primary ways that centers maintain partnerships with other entities.

Consistent with fusion center views reported at the 2010 National Fusion Center Conference, officials in all 14 fusion centers we contacted stated that achieving and maintaining the baseline capabilities was key to sustaining their centers. By achieving and maintaining these capabilities, fusion centers should have the necessary structures, processes, and tools in place to support the gathering, processing, analysis, and dissemination of terrorism, homeland security, and law enforcement information as part of the national, integrated network. At the 2010 National Fusion Center Conference, fusion center directors reported that achieving the critical operational capabilities at each fusion center was necessary to ensure an effective flow of information throughout the national network of fusion centers.[22] To do so, these directors cited the importance of performing baseline capability self-assessments, identifying gaps between operations and the baseline capabilities, developing plans to address the gaps, and leveraging existing resources more effectively and efficiently to close those gaps. For example, assessing gaps in centers' current information technology and communication infrastructure and the associated costs of implementing the necessary systems may enable fusion centers to focus resources more efficiently to address these needs and close the identified gaps. Officials in all of the 14 fusion centers we contacted said that, in

---

[22]This information was reported to PM-ISE, DHS, and DOJ by fusion center directors at the 2010 National Fusion Center Conference.

recognizing the importance of meeting the baseline capabilities, they had taken some steps to review their own operations and identify gaps between their current operations and the recommended baseline capabilities. For example, an official in one center said that he had conducted a systematic gap analysis of the center's current operations against the baseline capabilities and determined that the center still had to achieve an estimated 80 percent of the capabilities, such as developing performance metrics and an outreach program. Gaps identified by officials at the 14 fusion centers included, for example, the need to develop information technology and related tools for analysis; not having a privacy and civil liberties policy in place; not having identified a privacy/civil liberties officer; and not having identified a security officer.

To provide data about the baseline capabilities of fusion centers nationwide, the PM-ISE, DHS, and DOJ are conducting an ongoing systematic assessment of centers' capabilities. The goal of the nationwide assessment, according to DHS senior officials, is to help enable both federal and fusion center representatives to (1) obtain more accurate information on the current status of centers' abilities to meet the baseline capabilities, (2) help identify gaps between centers' current operations and the capabilities, and (3) use this information to develop strategies and realign resources to support centers' efforts to close those gaps going forward. Further, according to both DHS senior officials and fusion center representatives, the results of the assessment are also intended to provide centers with the information needed to develop more accurate and specific investment justifications to their SAAs in competing for DHS HSGP funding.

According to DHS and a senior official from the NFCA, personnel from DHS, the PM-ISE, and DOJ coordinated with state and local government representatives and fusion center officials prior to and during the National Fusion Center Conference in February 2010 to jointly identify four critical operational capabilities and four enabling capabilities to be prioritized in developing the national network of fusion centers.[23] Among the four enabling capabilities are those that relate to establishing a sustainment strategy and establishing privacy and civil liberties protections, as shown in table 2.

---

[23]Senior DHS officials stated that while these eight capabilities have been identified as the most critical of the baseline capabilities to achieve and maintain, the remaining capabilities are also to be accomplished and will be subsequently prioritized.

Table 2: Four Critical Operational Capabilities and Four Enabling Capabilities Identified by Fusion Centers and Federal Personnel at the 2010 National Fusion Center Conference

Operational capabilities
Ability to receive classified and unclassified information from federal partners
Ability to assess local implications of threat information through the use of a formal risk assessment process
Ability to further disseminate threat information to other state, local, tribal, territorial, and private sector entities within their jurisdiction
Ability to gather locally generated information, aggregate it, analyze it, and share it with federal partners as appropriate
Enabling capabilities[a]
Sustainment Strategy
Privacy and Civil Rights/Civil Liberties
Communications and Outreach
Security and Clearances

Source: DHS.

[a]Enabling capabilities are those that support the administrative and management functions of a fusion center.

The nationwide assessment of fusion centers consists of two phases—a self-report survey followed by onsite validation. First, the PM-ISE sent a self-assessment questionnaire, which was to be completed in May 2010, to all 72 designated fusion centers to use to assess their current operations against all baseline capabilities. Second, starting in June 2010, seven validation teams consisting of federal and fusion center personnel began making site visits to fusion centers to validate centers' responses to the self-assessment.[24] Specifically, the validation teams are to conduct a review of the four critical operational capabilities that were identified collaboratively by federal officials and fusion center directors as being critical to the functioning of the national network. Validation teams are also to review information on the privacy and civil liberties protections established by these fusion centers and to discuss the centers' sustainment strategies. Senior DHS officials stated that this review is to involve discussions on each fusion centers' experiences and related issues, challenges, and associated costs of achieving and maintaining the four critical operational capabilities, as well as the privacy and civil rights/civil

---

[24]Each validation team consists of personnel from DHS, DOJ, and the PM-ISE, as well as one fusion center director.

liberties enabling capability, to provide additional information on why gaps may exist and how to address them.

According to DHS senior officials, the site visits were completed in September 2010. The results of the assessment, which are to include the aggregate of both the self-assessment and on-site validation data, are expected to be analyzed and shared in a report with the participating fusion centers by the end of October 2010. Further, according to DHS senior officials, they are planning to conduct the assessment on a recurring basis. Thus, this initial assessment is expected to serve as a baseline against which to measure the development of the baseline capabilities in individual fusion centers, as well as across the national network.[25]

DHS Has Efforts Under Way to Link DHS Grants to Filling Baseline Capabilities Gaps and Plans to Assess Costs of the Fusion Center Network

DHS has opportunities to better target federal fusion center funding to fill critical baseline capability gaps and is taking steps to do so. Both the National Strategy and DHS emphasize that federal agencies are to play an active role in addressing the challenge of sustaining fusion centers by ensuring that they are able to achieve and maintain the baseline capabilities. Specifically, the National Strategy states that federal agencies are to assist fusion centers in incorporating the baseline capabilities into their operations by amending and modifying grants and grants guidance, and other applicable funding programs, to ensure that centers are able to meet and sustain the baseline capabilities and operational standards. In its fiscal year 2010 HSGP grant guidance, DHS encourages, but does not require, that fusion centers prioritize the allocation of HSGP funding they receive through their SAAs to meet and maintain the baseline capabilities. Further, senior DHS officials stated, generally, that the results of the nationwide assessment will be used to address future fusion center funding and that the office will determine how it may leverage DHS's HSGP to ensure that centers have access to grant funds and assist with putting these mechanisms in place for the future.

Senior officials from DHS as well as all 14 of the fusion centers we contacted stated that linking, or tying, future HSGP grant funding to achieving and maintaining the baseline capabilities may better enable

---

[25]According to a senior DHS I&A official, they have not determined how often (e.g., annually or every other year) the assessment will be conducted. They will make a determination using an after-action review of the results of the assessment and the related costs of administering it.

fusion centers to obtain the resources needed to address the gaps in baseline capabilities by allowing them to more specifically detail how grant funding is to be used in their investment justifications. For example, by tying future grant funding to developing fusion centers' ability to gather information, aggregate it, analyze it, and share it as appropriate, centers may be more likely to obtain the funding necessary to develop the specific information systems and analytical tools needed to enable them to achieve these capabilities. An Acting Director with FEMA's Office of Counterterrorism and Security Preparedness stated that, as part of developing the Fiscal Year 2011 HSGP guidance, FEMA is currently working with DHS and fusion center stakeholders to evaluate the potential for amending the guidance to accomplish two goals. Specifically, they are working to (1) require, rather than encourage, that fusion centers use 2011 grant funding allocated from SAAs to achieve and maintain all of the baseline capabilities; and (2) focus funding to specifically address gaps in baseline capabilities identified during the assessment process. For example, the official said that they are exploring options such as requiring centers to include in their investment justifications the results of the nationwide assessment and indicating how the center would use funding to fill any identified gaps. Further, this official added that FEMA has also begun collaborating within DHS and with DOJ to discuss current grant programs and possibilities for future interagency coordination on the support specifically for fusion centers. Directives such as these could help ensure that capabilities are met by enabling fusion centers to provide specific data about operational gaps and needs in their investment justifications.

While DHS could ensure that fusion centers target the federal funding they receive on filling baseline capabilities gaps, fusion centers have called on the federal government to establish a dedicated funding stream for them. DHS's HSGP is the primary grant program through which fusion centers receive funding, but these grants are not specifically focused on, nor limited to, fusion centers. As such, fusion centers compete with other state homeland security, law enforcement, and emergency management agencies and missions for a portion of the total amount of HSGP funding awarded to the SAA, which decides what portion of the total funding centers will receive. This process has generated long-standing concerns by the fusion center community about the lack of a longer-term, predictable funding source for the centers. For example, we reported in October 2007 that fusion centers reported challenges with funding, that these issues made it difficult to plan for the future, and that fusion centers were concerned about their ability to sustain their capability for the long term.[26] The Congressional Research Service (CRS) similarly reported in January 2008 that the threat of diminished or eliminated federal or state funding, such as a decrease in DHS grant funding programs, poses a risk to the development of fusion centers.[27] The DHS Office of Inspector General subsequently reported in December 2008 that fusion center officials they spoke with remained concerned with sustainability and funding, emphasizing that sustainment planning and funding from the federal government is essential for the success of fusion centers.[28]

Officials from 13 of the 14 centers we contacted cited a number of challenges with obtaining funding and the lack of a dedicated funding source, which affected their ability to plan long term or expand their operations.[29] For example, officials in 9 of these centers stated that uncertainty around the amount of federal grant funding the fusion center will receive from their states each year made it difficult to plan and expand operations. For instance, an official from a fusion center stated that the center relies on federal funding for 80 percent of its annual operating budget, but has to compete with several other state agencies and about 75 counties for a portion of HSGP funding each year. Officials in another fusion center stated that competition for limited federal grant funding has made getting the necessary funding more difficult and, as a result, they have had to scale back part of their outreach efforts to state and local entities, which is one of the four critical enabling capabilities.

In referring to the role fusion centers are to have in the national information sharing network, officials from all 14 fusion centers stated that there should be a federal grant funding stream or program dedicated specifically to support fusion centers. For example, officials from 6

---

[26]GAO-08-35.

[27]CRS, *Fusion Centers: Issues and Options for Congress*, RL34070 (Washington, D.C., Jan. 18, 2008).

[28]DHS OIG, *DHS' Role in State and Local Fusion Centers Is Evolving*, OIG-09-12 (Washington, D.C., Dec. 10, 2008).

[29]An official from the remaining fusion center stated that, while obtaining federal funding has not been challenging for his center, he believed that funding across the national network of centers is a big challenge and stated that, in his opinion, not having a dedicated funding program has negatively affected fusion centers efforts to effectively plan their operations.

centers stated that, since the National Strategy has identified fusion centers as a key component of the success of the ISE, the federal government should recognize the importance of providing dedicated funding support so that centers with varying missions and resources can continue to close baseline capability gaps and function as key partners in the national network. An official from one of these fusion centers stated that while centers are owned and operated by state and local entities—and should thus be supported by state and local resources—centers are also expected, as members of the ISE, to support a national information sharing, homeland security mission. Moreover, this official said that if fusion centers, as the primary focal points of information sharing between state and local and federal governments, are to support this mission, there should be a targeted federal funding source to support centers' efforts to meet and achieve the baseline capabilities, which have been identified as being essential for centers to function in the national network.

Senior I&A and FEMA officials said that they understood the fusion centers' concerns and recognized the challenges centers faced in competing for funding. However, these FEMA officials stated that they do not have the authority to create a fusion-center-specific grant within the HSGP and that doing so would require congressional action. These FEMA officials said that, in addition to the nationwide assessment that is underway to identify gaps in baseline capabilities, within the HSGP, they have broadened the allowable costs for which fusion centers can use HSGP funding and prioritized funding on achieving the baseline capabilities. However, DHS has not directed that a certain percentage of HSGP funding be used for fusion centers out of concern that other state agencies, such as emergency management agencies, would likewise lobby for such specific funding. These officials added that this would not be possible because they are trying to balance ensuring that SAAs have flexibility in administering HSGP funds while ensuring that federal fusion center requirements are supported and met.

Further, senior DHS officials stated that DHS has recognized the need to conduct extensive research on funding options for fusion centers, stating that, after the nationwide assessment is completed, the SLPO is to assess key budgetary processes to determine how support to fusion centers can be affected and determine DHS's ability to identify additional funding options for centers. In addition, Fiscal Year 2012 implementation guidance for the ISE requires that, by October 29, 2010, DHS should develop and promulgate an annual common reporting process that will document the total operational and sustainment costs of each of the 72 fusion centers in the national network. Senior DHS officials stated that, while not yet completed, the SLPO has begun to develop this reporting process and that it is to be based in part on surveys implemented in previous years at fusion centers. These officials added that the goal of the guidance is to develop annual data on the costs to sustain fusion centers, and that these data are a necessary first step to assessing the adequacy of current funding mechanisms.

Taking Steps to Implement Standard Performance Measures to Track the Results of Fusion Centers' Efforts to Support Information Sharing Could Help Demonstrate Centers' Value to the ISE

If fusion centers are to receive continued financial support, it is important that centers are also able to demonstrate that they are providing critical information that is helping the federal government and state and local agencies protect against terrorist and homeland security threats. We have previously emphasized the importance of performance measures as management tools to track an agency's progress toward achieving goals and to provide information on which to base organizational and management decisions.[30] Performance data allow agencies to share effective approaches, recognize problems, look for solutions, and develop ways to improve results.

The Fusion Center Guidelines recommend that individual fusion centers develop and use performance measures as an ongoing means to measure and track performance and determine and evaluate the effectiveness of their operations to make better decisions and allocate resources. The Baseline Capabilities expand on these guidelines and recommend that fusion centers develop measures that allow them to, among other things, track their performance and results against the centers' individual goals and objectives. Officials from 5 of the 14 centers we contacted stated that one of the gaps they identified between their current operations and the baseline capabilities was development of methods to monitor and evaluate their fusion center's performance.[31] Officials from these 5 fusion centers stated that it was a challenge to develop performance measures to monitor their operations and demonstrate results because their mission was to prevent crimes, and it is difficult to know how many crimes were averted due to their efforts. Additionally, officials from 3 of these 5 fusion centers stated that their ability to develop performance measures was also

---

[30]GAO, *Executive Guide: Effectively Implementing the Government Performance and Results Act*, GAO/GGD-96-118 (Washington, D.C.: June 1996).

[31]Because we asked fusion center officials about baseline capability gaps in general, not about gaps in performance metrics specifically, not all fusion center officials provided information on their status of developing performance measures.

affected by the fact that, due to limited personnel, addressing other operational work responsibilities, such as analyzing intelligence information and developing related reports, was the priority. A senior official from NFCA said that these challenges are similarly experienced across the broader network of fusion centers, and that centers would welcome a collaborative process in developing these measures to involve participation from, among others, federal agencies such as DHS, DOJ, and the PM-ISE.

According to DHS senior officials, the nationwide assessment currently under way is to gauge whether or not each fusion center has developed methods to monitor and evaluate its own performance. For example, the assessment results are to indicate to what extent a center has developed mechanisms to receive feedback on the value of its products or to determine the effectiveness of its operations in achieving identified goals and objectives. DHS senior officials stated that the results will be used to help federal agencies assess to what extent there are gaps in this baseline capability across the national network of fusion centers and to make decisions about where to allocate resources to support centers' efforts to develop these individual performance measures.

However, while federal guidance recommends that individual fusion centers develop and use performance measures as a baseline capability, currently there are no standard measures to track performance across fusion centers and demonstrate the impact of centers' operations in support of national information sharing goals. According to PM-ISE and DHS senior officials, the results of the nationwide assessment are not intended to provide standard measures for fusion centers to demonstrate the results they are achieving in meeting broader information sharing goals as part of the national network. For example, the assessment results are not intended to provide information about how well centers disseminated federal information to local security partners or how useful federal agencies found the information that centers provided them.

The PM-ISE and DHS have recognized the value of implementing standard performance measures across fusion centers. In its 2009 annual report to Congress, the PM-ISE stated that among the activities the office would undertake in 2009 and 2010 would be designing a set of performance measures to demonstrate the value of a national integrated network of fusion centers operating in accordance with the baseline capabilities. Senior PM-ISE officials stated that the PM-ISE had not begun this effort and is no longer planning to develop these performance measures however, because DHS, as the lead agency in coordinating federal support of fusion centers, is now responsible for managing development of these performance measures. Further, in response to a requirement under the 9/11 Commission Act, DHS stated in its 2008 fusion center Concept of Operations that it will develop qualitative and quantitative measures of performance for the overall network of fusion centers and relevant federal entities, such as DHS and DOJ.[32] According to senior DHS officials, the agency recognizes that developing these measures is important to demonstrate the value of agency efforts in support of the ISE. However, these officials stated that, while DHS has started collecting some information that will help in developing such measures, the agency is currently focusing on completing the nationwide assessment to gauge the capabilities and gaps across fusion centers.[33] As such, these officials said that they have not defined next steps or target timeframes for designing and implementing these measures. Standard practices for program and project management state that specific desired outcomes or results should be conceptualized, defined, and documented in the planning process as part of a road map, along with the appropriate steps and time frames needed to achieve those results.[34] By defining the steps it will take to design and implement a set of standard measures to track the results and performance across fusion centers and committing to a target timeframe for completion, DHS could help ensure that centers and federal agencies demonstrate the value of fusion centers' operations to national information sharing goals and prioritize limited resources needed to achieve and maintain those functions deemed critical to support the national fusion center network.

---

[32]Ninety days after enactment of the 9/11 Commission Act, and before it implemented the fusion center initiative, DHS was required, in consultation with others, to submit a concept of operations for the fusion center initiative that contained a developed set of quantitative metrics to measure program output and a developed set of quantitative instruments to assess the extent to which stakeholders believe their needs are being addressed, among other things. Pub. L. No. 110-53, § 511(d). The plan submitted did not contain the developed set of metrics and acknowledged the Baseline Capabilities was the framework from which measures of effectiveness for fusion centers could be developed.

[33]For example, one senior DHS official stated that the agency has begun collecting and aggregating information on fusion center "success stories" as examples of the contributions centers provide to the ISE.

[34]Project Management Institute, *The Standard for Program Management* © (2006).

Federal Agencies Are Providing Technical Assistance and Training to Centers to Help Them Develop Privacy and Civil Liberties Policies and Protections, and DHS Is Assessing the Status of These Protections

DHS and DOJ are providing technical assistance to assist fusion centers in developing privacy and civil liberties policies, and fusion centers nationwide are in varying stages of completing their policies. Additionally, fusion center officials we interviewed reported taking steps to designate privacy/civil liberties officials and conduct outreach about their policies. Further, DHS and DOJ are providing training to fusion centers on implementing privacy and civil liberties policies and protections that officials in the 14 centers we contacted found helpful and wanted to be continued. DHS also has several efforts underway to assess the status of fusion centers' privacy and civil liberties protections, including updating the privacy and civil liberties impact assessments to help ensure centers' protections are implemented.

DHS and DOJ Are Providing Technical Assistance to Help Fusion Centers Develop Privacy and Civil Liberties Policies, and Centers Nationwide Are in Varying Stages of Completing Their Policies

Because fusion centers are collecting and sharing information on individuals, federal law establishes requirements and federal agencies have issued guidelines for fusion centers to establish policies that address privacy and civil liberties issues. Consistent with the 9/11 Commission Act, the Fusion Center Guidelines call for fusion centers to develop, publish, and adhere to a privacy and civil liberties policy. Further, the Baseline Capabilities provide more specific guidance on developing such a policy and contain a set of recommended procedures for fusion centers to include in their policies to ensure that their centers' operations are conducted in a manner that protects the privacy, civil liberties, and other legal rights of individuals according to applicable federal and state law. According to federal guidance, if centers adhere to the Baseline Capabilities, they in turn will be in adherence with the ISE Privacy Guidelines. Further, DHS's fiscal year 2010 HSGP funding guidance stipulates that federal funds may not be used to support fusion-center-related initiatives unless a fusion center has developed a privacy and civil liberties policy containing protections that are at least as comprehensive as the ISE Privacy Guidelines within 6 months of the grant award. According to senior DHS Privacy officials, the fiscal year 2010 grants were awarded in September 2010, so fusion centers will have until March 2011 to have their policies reviewed and certified by the DHS Privacy Office. If a fusion center does not have a certified privacy and civil liberties policy by March 2011, according to DHS guidance, DHS grants funds may only be used to support the development or completion of the center's privacy and civil liberties protection requirements.

To facilitate fusion centers meeting federal requirements for their privacy and civil liberties policies, DHS and DOJ have published a template and established a process to review and certify the policies. The template incorporates the primary components of the ISE Privacy Guidelines and provides sample language for the center to use as a starting point when drafting procedures for a privacy and civil liberties policy. To ensure fusion centers comply with the certification requirements in DHS's grant guidance, DHS and DOJ have established a joint process to review and certify fusion centers' privacy and civil liberties policies. First, a fusion center sends its draft policy to a team of attorneys contracted by DOJ's Bureau of Justice Assistance to provide a detailed review of the policy and compare its language and provisions against language in the template. After its review, DOJ submits the center's completed draft policy to the DHS Privacy Office for a final review. This office reviews the policy specifically to determine whether it contains protections that are at least as comprehensive as the ISE Privacy Guidelines. If the policy satisfies the ISE Privacy Guidelines, the DHS Chief Privacy Officer sends written notification to the fusion center director stating that the policy has been certified.

Using this guidance and technical assistance, fusion centers nationwide are in varying stages of completing their privacy and civil liberties policies. Specifically, 21 centers had certified policies; 33 centers had submitted policies; and 18 centers, while they have not yet submitted their policies, were currently receiving technical assistance, as of August 2010.[35] Senior DHS Privacy officials stated that they expect that all 72 fusion centers will have submitted their policies and the federal agencies will be able to review and certify them by the March 2011 deadline to avoid any limits on grant funding. The 14 centers we contacted were at different stages of the review process and reported that they found the template and technical assistance to be helpful. Specifically, 7 centers had certified policies, 6 had

---

[35]The 21 centers are: Ohio Strategic Analysis and Information Center; Louisiana State Analytic & Fusion Exchange; Vermont Fusion Center; Indiana Intelligence Fusion Center; Nevada Threat Analysis Center; Austin Regional Intelligence Center; Iowa Fusion Center; Georgia Information Sharing and Analysis Center; Statewide Terrorism and Intelligence Center (Illinois); Oklahoma Information Fusion Center; Washington State Fusion Center; Florida Fusion Center; Kansas City Regional Terrorism Early Warning Group Interagency Analysis Center; Houston Regional Information Sharing Center; Wisconsin Statewide Information Center; Southern Nevada Counter-Terrorism Center; California State Terrorism Threat Assessment Information Center; Northern California Regional Intelligence Center; San Diego Law Enforcement Coordination Center; Central California Intelligence Center; and Los Angeles Joint Regional Intelligence Center.

policies in the review process, and 1 center was drafting its policy. Officials from all 14 of the fusion centers stated that they used or were using the template to write their policies, and that the template was a helpful guide to developing their policies. In addition, officials in 13 of these centers that had submitted their policies for review stated that the technical assistance and guidance DHS and DOJ provided was integral in assisting them draft their policies, especially a tracking sheet the DOJ review team used to document comments, feedback, and recommendations.

Consistent with Recommended Federal Guidance, Fusion Center Officials We Interviewed Have Taken Steps to Designate Privacy/Civil Liberties Officials and Conduct Outreach

The Baseline Capabilities recommend that fusion centers designate a privacy/civil liberties official or a privacy committee to coordinate the development, implementation, maintenance, and oversight of the fusion center's privacy and civil liberties policies and procedures. Furthermore, the Baseline Capabilities recommend that if the designated privacy/civil liberties official is not an attorney, fusion centers should have access to legal counsel with the appropriate expertise to help clarify related laws, rules, regulations, and statutes to ensure that centers' operations are adhering to privacy and civil liberties protections. Officials from all 14 fusion centers we contacted stated that they have taken steps to designate privacy/civil liberties officials or form privacy committees. For example, officials in 12 of these centers said that they designated a single individual to serve as the privacy/civil liberties official; officials in 1 fusion center selected two officials—attorneys from the state's bureau of investigation and the state's department of safety; and officials in 1 center created a privacy committee. For more information on the qualifications of privacy/civil liberties officials and the challenges associated with designating them, see appendix I.

In addition to developing a privacy and civil liberties policy and designating a privacy/civil liberties official, the Baseline Capabilities recommend that fusion centers facilitate public awareness of their policy by making it available to the public. Officials in 7 of 14 fusion centers we contacted described taking steps to make the public aware of their fusion center's privacy and civil liberties protections.[36] For example, officials in 3 centers said that they met with privacy and civil liberties advocacy groups

---

[36]Because we asked fusion center officials about outreach and training in general in establishing privacy and civil liberties policies, protections, and plans, not about outreach to the public specifically, not all fusion center officials provided information on steps they may have taken in this particular area.

to elicit feedback about the centers' policies. For instance, one official said that his fusion center shared its policy with a local chapter of the ACLU, which reviewed it and made suggestions for revisions, some of which the center implemented. Additionally, officials from 6 of 14 fusion centers we interviewed said that they posted their policies on their centers' Web sites or planned to post them once they are certified. To assist centers with their outreach efforts, DHS and DOJ officials stated that they are developing a communications and outreach guidebook that will include information on how fusion centers can communicate their mission, operations, and privacy and civil liberties protections to state and local governments, privacy advocacy groups, and the general population. These officials added that this guidebook will recommend that fusion centers post their privacy and civil liberties policies online to help centers achieve the baseline capability of promoting transparency and public awareness of their privacy and civil liberties protections.

Fusion Center Officials We Interviewed Reported That DHS's and DOJ's Training on Privacy and Civil Liberties Protections Was Helpful and Would Like It Continued after Their Policies Are Developed

The 9/11 Commission Act requires DHS to establish guidelines for fusion centers that include standards for fusion centers to provide appropriate privacy training for all state, local, tribal, and private sector representatives at the fusion center, in coordination with DHS's Privacy Office and CRCL. To support fusion centers in this effort, DHS, in partnership with DOJ and Global, has implemented a three-part training and technical assistance program for fusion center personnel consisting of (1) a "Training the Trainers" Program, where representatives from DHS's Privacy Office and CRCL provide instruction to fusion center privacy/civil liberties officials with the intent that these officials then implement and teach the material to personnel at their centers; (2) a Web site "Tool Kit" or Web portal, which provides a single point of access to federal resources on privacy training and contains training material and video resources for state and local personnel on privacy topics; and (3) an On-site Training Program, where representatives from DHS's Privacy Office and CRCL travel to fusion centers, upon request, to provide training on privacy, civil rights, and civil liberties issues. Appendix II discusses this training program in greater detail.

Officials from all 14 fusion centers we contacted stated that DHS's and DOJ's three-part training and technical assistance program was helpful and expressed a need for continued training or guidance as they continue to establish their privacy and civil liberties protections. Fusion center officials cited several reasons why they wanted continued training and updated guidance, including evolving privacy laws, and the recognition that some privacy/civil liberties officials may lack privacy-related expertise or backgrounds. In addition to training, six fusion center officials expressed a need for continued privacy guidance, such as briefings on examples of fusion center privacy violations and how they were corrected. For example, an official from one of these centers expressed a need for federal guidance on how centers should deal with certain groups who make threats against state or local governments, as these groups can span across multiple states. Recognizing that fusion centers would like continued federal training and guidance on privacy, senior officials from DHS's Privacy Office and CRCL stated that they plan to continue the DHS-DOJ joint three-part training and technical assistance program over the next several years and to tailor its privacy, civil rights, and civil liberties instruction to the needs of individual centers. Further, senior DHS Privacy officials stated that a goal of the training program is to develop multiyear relationships with privacy/civil liberties officials in each center, helping to establish a professional cadre of trained privacy/civil liberties officials across the national fusion center network.

DHS Has Efforts Under Way to Assess the Status of Fusion Centers' Privacy and Civil Liberties Protections

Senior DHS Privacy officials stated that the review of fusion centers' privacy and civil liberties policies is a first step in providing ongoing federal oversight of the development of privacy and civil liberties protections across fusion centers. These officials stated that continued assessment and oversight—by the federal government and by fusion centers themselves—is necessary to ensure that the protections described in centers' policies are implemented in accordance with all applicable privacy regulations, laws, and constitutional protections. For example, a Director with DHS's Privacy Office noted that a fusion center can, in theory, have a model privacy and civil liberties policy but not correctly implement its protections, increasing the risk of potential violations such as the proliferation of inaccurate data. The 9/11 Commission Act requires that the Secretary issue guidelines that contain standards that fusion centers shall not only develop and publish a privacy and civil liberties policy, but also that they adhere to it. Further, the Baseline Capabilities recommend that fusion centers, as part of their privacy and civil liberties protections, identify methods for monitoring the implementation of their privacy and civil liberties policies and procedures to incorporate revisions and updates. While the 9/11 Commission Act does not dictate specific oversight mechanisms for fusion center privacy and civil liberties protections, DHS, in coordination with DOJ and the PM-ISE, has two efforts under way to assess the status of these protections across fusion centers and is taking steps to encourage centers to assess their own protections going forward to identify any existing privacy and civil liberties risks and develop strategies to mitigate them.

First, the nationwide assessment asks fusion centers to provide information on each of the privacy-related baseline capabilities, including information on the centers' designated privacy/civil liberties officials, components of their privacy and civil liberties policies and related protections, policy outreach efforts, and training. Following that, validation teams are to review the self-reported information in detail with each fusion center. According to senior DHS officials, this information may help to identify any critical gaps in privacy and civil liberties protections across the national network of fusion centers. Senior DHS Privacy officials stated that this information will be an important tool in developing a longer-term oversight and assessment strategy to ensure that resources are aligned to address these gaps.

Second, the 9/11 Commission Act, enacted in August 2007, requires, among other things, that DHS submit (1) a report within 90 days of the enactment of the Act containing a Concept of Operations for the Fusion Center Initiative that includes a privacy impact assessment (PIA) and a civil liberties impact assessment (CLIA) examining the privacy and civil liberties implications of fusion centers, and (2) another PIA and CLIA within 1 year of enactment.[37] In general, these assessments allow agencies to assess privacy and civil liberties risks in their information sharing initiatives and to identify potential corrective actions to address those risks. DHS published a PIA in December 2008[38] that identified several risks to privacy presented by fusion centers, explained mitigation strategies for those risks, and made recommendations on how DHS and fusion centers can take additional action to further enhance the privacy interests of the citizens in their jurisdictions.[39] CRCL similarly published a CLIA in

---

[37] According to DHS, the purpose of the State and Local Fusion Center Concept of Operations (CONOPs) was to establish a framework for a comprehensive, coordinated and consistent approach for outreach by DHS to fusion centers. DHS published its CONOPs in December 2008.

[38] DHS, *Privacy Impact Assessment for the Department of Homeland Security State, Local, and Regional Fusion Center Initiative* (Dec. 11, 2008).

[39] According to a Director with DHS's Privacy Office, the PIA was not published within the 90-day time period stated in the 9/11 Commission Act because the CONOPs, in which the initial PIA was required to be included, was itself not published until December 2008. This official added that, in addition, within this 90 day time period, many fusion centers were just beginning to establish their operations and, similarly, federal efforts to support and provide guidance to fusion centers on their privacy and civil liberties protections were also in the early stages. By delaying issuance of the initial PIA until December 2008, this official stated the DHS Privacy Office had more time to assess the privacy implications of the fusion center initiative.

December 2008 that evaluated fusion centers' impact on the civil liberties of particular groups or individuals, outlined procedures for filing a civil liberties complaint with DHS, and highlighted the importance of training fusion center personnel on civil rights and civil liberties.

DHS has not completed the second PIA or CLIA, which were to be issued by August 2008. However, according to senior DHS Privacy officials, the DHS Privacy Office is currently beginning to develop the updated PIA. These officials said that they identified two key milestones when determining when to begin work on the updated PIA. First, the officials said that they wanted to complete the "training the trainers" program for designated fusion center privacy/civil liberties officials, which they did in July 2010. Second, officials said that they delayed the start of the updated PIA to allow time for fusion centers to develop their privacy and civil liberties policies—which are to be certified by DHS by March 2011. Ensuring that centers had completed, and were beginning to implement, their policies would help in assessing updates to any risks identified in the initial PIA, according to these officials. Senior DHS Privacy officials stated that they have begun planning for the updated PIA, and that the assessment will be published in 2011. These officials stated that the updated PIA will be comprehensive in its scope, and include an assessment of the steps fusion centers have taken to address the recommendations of the 2008 PIA, an analysis of federal and state government involvement in fusion center privacy and civil liberties protections, a description of what federal agencies have done and are doing to assist fusion centers in establishing these protections, and a discussion about related initiatives. These officials added that the updated PIA will be a useful tool in assessing where fusion centers are in implementing protections and addressing the 2008 PIA recommendations, and that the information will be used to inform decisions on where to focus their training and oversight efforts going forward.

Further, senior officials from CRCL stated that they have also begun to develop the updated CLIA, and plan to publish the assessment in 2011. According to these officials, the updated CLIA will address topics such as oversight of fusion centers, common issues and challenges that fusion centers face in establishing civil rights and civil liberties protections, examples of civil rights and civil liberties complaints directed at fusion centers, and key issues brought up during fusion center trainings. Given the assessments' proposed scope and content, completing the updates to the PIA and CLIA as required will help provide critical information to help ensure that fusion centers are implementing privacy and civil liberties protections and that DHS, and other federal agencies, are supporting them in their efforts.

In addition to the nationwide assessment and updated PIA and CLIA, DHS is also taking steps to encourage fusion centers to conduct their own PIAs once their privacy and civil liberties policies are reviewed and certified by the DHS Privacy Office as a means to oversee their own privacy and civil liberties protections going forward. According to senior DHS Privacy officials, individual PIAs are integral for a fusion center's development and promote transparency by describing fusion center activities and authorities more fully than the policies can alone. To assist fusion centers in developing their own PIAs, DHS and DOJ jointly published a guide to conducting PIAs specific to state, local, and tribal information sharing initiatives, including a template to lead policy developers through appropriate privacy risk assessment questions.[40] In addition to the template itself, according to senior DHS Privacy officials, the importance of conducting a fusion center PIA is conveyed through the three-part training and technical assistance program where the steps the office took to conduct its own PIA in 2008 are covered.

Conclusions

Fusion centers—as the primary focal points for the two-way exchange of information between federal agencies and state and local governments—play a critical and unique role in national efforts to combat terrorism more effectively. In light of their reliance on fusion centers as critical components in the ISE, DHS, in collaboration with DOJ and the PM-ISE, provide fusion centers with a variety of support, including DHS grant funding, personnel, and technical assistance. However, centers remain concerned about their long-term sustainability and ability to meet and maintain the baseline capabilities given the current federal funding sources and fiscally constrained state and local economic environments. DHS's efforts to require, rather than encourage, centers to target HSGP funding to achieving and maintaining the baseline capabilities are aimed at enabling fusion centers to close gaps in capabilities and develop more accurate and specific investment justifications in competing for DHS HSGP funding within their respective states. Further, by completing the nationwide assessment and the required cost assessment of the fusion center network, DHS can begin to address long-standing concerns and

[40]DHS and DOJ (Global), *Guide to Conducting Privacy Impact Assessments for State, Local, and Tribal Information Sharing Initiatives.*

questions about sustaining the fusion center network. If fusion centers are to receive continued financial support, it is important that centers demonstrate that they are providing critical information that is helping the federal government protect against homeland security and terrorist threats through a set of performance measures. The PM-ISE and DHS have recognized the value of developing such performance measures, but defining the steps it will take to design and implement them and committing to a target time frame for completion could help ensure that fusion centers and federal agencies track fusion center performance in a manner that demonstrates the value of fusion center operations within the ISE.

Recommendation for Executive Action

To enhance the ability to demonstrate the results fusion centers are achieving in support of national information sharing goals and help prioritize how future resources should be allocated, we recommend that the Secretary of Homeland Security direct the State and Local Program Office, in partnership with fusion center officials, to define the steps it will take to design and implement a set of standard performance measures to show the results and value centers are adding to the Information Sharing Environment and commit to a target timeframe for completing them.

Agency Comments and Our Evaluation

We requested comments on a draft of this report from the Secretary of Homeland Security, the Attorney General, and the Program Manager for the ISE on September 13, 2010. DHS, DOJ, and the PM-ISE did not provide official written comments to include in our report. However, in an email received September 23, 2010, a DHS liaison stated that DHS concurred with our recommendation. DHS and DOJ provided written technical comments, which we incorporated into the report, as appropriate. In its technical comments, DHS stated that the agency has recently started to develop a performance management framework to demonstrate the value and impact of the national network of fusion centers and is using the nationwide assessment data to support the development of specific performance measures. With regard to target timeframes, DHS stated that it is planning to (1) collaborate with fusion center directors and interagency partners on the development of these performance measures throughout the remainder of 2010 and (2) provide performance management resources at the next National Fusion Center Conference in March 2011. If properly implemented and monitored, developing these standard performance measures should enhance the ability to demonstrate the results fusion centers are achieving in support of national information sharing goals and help prioritize how future resources should be allocated.

DHS also noted that while the report emphasizes the importance of sustainment funding for fusion centers, it does not recommend that DHS develop a sustainment strategy to assist fusion centers in getting the critical federal support they require. In our 2007 report, we recommended that the federal government articulate such a sustainment strategy for fusion centers—a recommendation with which DHS agreed and that we consider to still be current and applicable. Specifically, we recommended that the federal government define and articulate its role in supporting fusion centers and determine whether it expects to provide resources to centers over the long-term to help ensure their sustainability. During our review, DHS described actions that it plans to take that begin to build this strategy. More specifically, DHS said that it plans to collect and assess cost data from centers—a necessary first step to assessing the adequacy of current funding mechanisms and level of the resources that DHS provides to fusion centers. While a positive start, it will be important for DHS to follow through on these plans and develop a sustainment strategy for fusion centers. This would in turn be responsive to our recommendation.

We are sending copies of this report to the Secretary of Homeland Security, the Attorney General, the Program Manager for the ISE, and other interested congressional committees and subcommittees. In addition, this report will be available at no charge on GAO's Web site at http://www.gao.gov.

If you or your staff have any questions concerning this report or wish to discuss the matter further, please contact me at (202) 512-8777, or larencee@gao.gov. Contact points for our Offices of Congressional Relations and Public Affairs may be found on the last page of this report. Key contributors to this report are listed in appendix III.

Eileen Regen Larence
Director, Homeland Security
and Justice Issues

Appendix I: Qualifications of Fusion Center Privacy/Civil Liberties Officials and Challenges Associated with Designating Them

According to our interviews with officials in 14 fusion centers, the individuals designated to be privacy/civil liberties officials varied in terms of their position and legal experience. For example, in the 13 fusion centers with privacy/civil liberties officials, 3 of these officials were center directors and 6 were analysts. The remaining 4 fusion centers designated attorneys from other bureaus or agencies within their respective state or local governments, such as state attorneys' general offices, as their privacy/civil liberties official. These officials stated that because they either did not have the appropriate legal expertise within the fusion center or had an existing working relationship with a state bureau or agency, designating officials outside their center as the privacy/civil liberties official was the best option available in achieving this baseline capability. Among the 9 centers that had designated fusion center personnel as the privacy/civil liberties official, none of these personnel was an attorney; however, officials in 3 of these centers stated that their privacy/civil liberties officials had access to other legal counsel within the state police agency or city police department, for example, to help clarify laws and regulations governing privacy and civil liberties protections and to assist with the development of the centers' policies.

Fusion center officials we interviewed reported several challenges in designating privacy/civil liberties officials, including concerns that some officials had other operational duties at the fusion center or may not have sufficient legal expertise to ensure implementation of privacy and civil liberties protections. For example, of the nine fusion centers with directors or analysts serving as the privacy/civil liberties official, two had officials whose sole duty was to oversee development of the center's privacy and civil liberties policy and implementation of privacy and civil liberties protections. The other seven privacy/civil liberties officials had other operational duties at the fusion center. For instance, one fusion center's privacy/civil liberties official also served as the center's critical infrastructure and key resources analyst, which according to the center officials, slowed the development of the center's privacy and civil liberties policy. According to a Director with DHS's Privacy Office, it is difficult to assess the effect of fusion center privacy/civil liberties officials having responsibilities outside of their privacy-related duties because the position is relatively new and this is common. The official added that, in general, it is better to have the designated privacy/civil liberties official be able to focus exclusively on privacy-related duties. Additionally, officials in two fusion centers were concerned that their privacy/civil liberties officials may not have sufficient legal expertise to effectively monitor privacy and civil liberties protections at the centers. For example, one official stated that it was difficult to identify personnel who, in addition to legal expertise, had experience in both intelligence analysis and standard law enforcement practices which, in his experience, were necessary skills for a center's privacy/civil liberties official. Senior DHS Privacy officials said that, in recognizing that fusion center privacy/civil liberties officials have multiple duties and vary in terms of their experience and legal expertise, DHS is committed to training and has taken steps to train centers' designated officials and tailor DHS's privacy instruction to the needs of individual fusion centers to help centers achieve this baseline capability.

Appendix II: Privacy/Civil Rights and Civil Liberties Training and Technical Assistance Program

DHS, in partnership with DOJ and Global, has implemented a three-part training and technical assistance program in support of fusion centers' efforts to provide appropriate privacy, civil rights, and civil liberties training for all state, local, tribal, and private sector representatives at the fusion center:

- A "Training the Trainers" Program: In this 2010 program, representatives from the DHS Privacy Office and CRCL provided instruction to fusion center privacy/civil liberties officials at four regional fusion center conferences that are held annually. These 1 1/2-day classes were intended to provide privacy/civil liberties officials with instruction on the requirements of a fusion center in implementing privacy and civil liberties protections, the general privacy law framework of the ISE, and instruction on how privacy/civil liberties officials can best teach the material to fusion center personnel at their centers. According to senior officials from CRCL, privacy/civil liberties officials from 68 of 72 fusion centers have received the training as of August 2010.[1] According to directors with the DHS Privacy Office and CRCL, the training delivered at the conferences is specialized and tailored based on feedback the offices receive from fusion center staff on key issues they would like covered. Officials added that they obtain feedback at each training session to also identify the privacy, civil rights, and civil liberties-related subject areas in which privacy/civil liberties officials may need more training. Participants in this program are asked to teach the material to other fusion center personnel within their centers within 6 months.
- A Web site "Tool Kit:" This tool-kit, or Web portal, provides a single point of access to federal resources on privacy, civil rights, and civil liberties training. The portal contains training material and video resources for state and local personnel on a broad range of privacy, civil rights, and civil liberties topics. The public Web portal can be found at www.it.ojp.gov/PrivacyLiberty. Furthermore, the Web portal provides access to training resources on the requirements in 28 C.F.R. part 23, which contains guidelines for law enforcement agencies operating

---

[1]To train privacy/civil liberties officials from the fusion centers who were not able to attend the regional conferences, CRCL scheduled a fifth "Training the Trainers" session, which was held in August 2010.

federally grant-funded criminal intelligence systems.[2] DHS HSGP guidance states that in fiscal year 2010, all fusion center employees are expected to complete the online 28 C.F.R. part 23 certification training. Officials from all 14 fusion centers we contacted stated that fusion center staff have completed the requisite online certification training, and that it was helpful in making their staff aware of the regulations governing their criminal intelligence systems. Furthermore, officials from 5 of these 14 fusion centers stated that they plan to require that fusion center personnel complete the 28 C.F.R. part 23 certification training on an annual basis to ensure that staff are well-versed on privacy requirements.

- An On-site Training Program: For this program, representatives from the DHS Privacy Office and CRCL travel to fusion centers, upon request, to provide a full day of training on privacy, civil rights, and civil liberties issues in the following core areas: civil rights and civil liberties basics in the ISE, privacy fundamentals, cultural competency, First Amendment issues in the ISE, and "red flags" when reviewing or creating intelligence products. Additionally, fusion centers have the option of selecting topics from a list of available training modules, such as a civil rights and civil liberties case scenario or an intelligence analysis product review exercise, and receiving customized instruction based on the training needs of their fusion center. Prior to the training, representatives from CRCL conduct interviews with fusion center officials to learn about their specific privacy, civil rights and civil liberties questions or issues, review state constitution and relevant state law, and research local media to identify the types of issues related to the work of the fusion center that have raised concerns among citizens in their jurisdictions. According to senior officials from the DHS Privacy Office and CRCL, as of August 2010, 21 of 72 fusion centers have received this on-site training. Officials we contacted in 3 fusion centers stated that they had requested and received on-site training on privacy, civil rights, and civil liberties protections from DHS personnel at their fusion centers and that the training was helpful.

---

[2]The standards contained at 28 C.F.R. part 23 apply to federally funded criminal intelligence systems. As described by the regulations, because the intelligence data collected and exchanged could pose potential threats to the privacy of individuals to whom the data relates, guidelines are required. 28 C.F.R. § 23.2. Accordingly, criminal intelligence sharing systems may only disseminate criminal intelligence information to law enforcement agencies that agree to follow procedures consistent with enumerated principles, such as sanctions against unauthorized access and storing information such that it cannot be modified without authorization, among others. 28 C.F.R. § 23.3.

Appendix III: GAO Contact and Staff Acknowledgments

GAO Contact

Eileen R. Larence, (202) 512-8777 or larencee@gao.gov

Acknowledgments

In addition to the contact named above, Mary Catherine Hult, Assistant Director; Hugh Paquette; Kevin Craw; Katherine Davis; John de Ferrari; Matt Grote; David Plocher; Michael Silver; and Janet Temko made key contributions to this report.

GAO's Mission	The Government Accountability Office, the audit, evaluation, and investigative arm of Congress, exists to support Congress in meeting its constitutional responsibilities and to help improve the performance and accountability of the federal government for the American people. GAO examines the use of public funds; evaluates federal programs and policies; and provides analyses, recommendations, and other assistance to help Congress make informed oversight, policy, and funding decisions. GAO's commitment to good government is reflected in its core values of accountability, integrity, and reliability.
Obtaining Copies of GAO Reports and Testimony	The fastest and easiest way to obtain copies of GAO documents at no cost is through GAO's Web site (www.gao.gov). Each weekday afternoon, GAO posts on its Web site newly released reports, testimony, and correspondence. To have GAO e-mail you a list of newly posted products, go to www.gao.gov and select "E-mail Updates."
Order by Phone	The price of each GAO publication reflects GAO's actual cost of production and distribution and depends on the number of pages in the publication and whether the publication is printed in color or black and white. Pricing and ordering information is posted on GAO's Web site, http://www.gao.gov/ordering.htm. Place orders by calling (202) 512-6000, toll free (866) 801-7077, or TDD (202) 512-2537. Orders may be paid for using American Express, Discover Card, MasterCard, Visa, check, or money order. Call for additional information.
To Report Fraud, Waste, and Abuse in Federal Programs	Contact: Web site: www.gao.gov/fraudnet/fraudnet.htm E-mail: fraudnet@gao.gov Automated answering system: (800) 424-5454 or (202) 512-7470
Congressional Relations	Ralph Dawn, Managing Director, dawnr@gao.gov, (202) 512-4400 U.S. Government Accountability Office, 441 G Street NW, Room 7125 Washington, DC 20548
Public Affairs	Chuck Young, Managing Director, youngc1@gao.gov, (202) 512-4800 U.S. Government Accountability Office, 441 G Street NW, Room 7149 Washington, DC 20548